USING MATHS

DINOSAUR DIG

Wendy Clemson and Frances Clemson

First published in 2007 in Great Britain by ticktock Media Ltd.,

Unit 2, Orchard Business Centre, North Farm Road, Tunbridge Wells, Kent TN2 3XF, Great Britain.

A CIP catalogue record for this book is available from the British Library.

ISBN 978 1 84696 060 4

Printed in China.

ticktock project editor: Rebecca Clunes
ticktock project designer: Sara Greasley

Picture Credits
t=top, b=bottom, c=centre, l=left, r=right, f=far

1, 2, 3FR, 26B, 27T, 31T Lisa Alderson. 3FL, 3L, 3C, 3R, 6L, 6R, 17, 14BCL, 14BFR, 14BCR, 34T, 26T, 29B, 31B, 32 Simon Mendez.
5, 6C, 7B, 8L, 11B, 21, 23, 29T, 30 Luis Rey. 4TL, 4BL, 4TR, 8-9, 9T, 15B, 20, 27CL, 27C, 28T, 28L Shutterstock. 4BR BananaStock/Alamy.
14T David R. Frazier Photolibrary, Inc./Alamy. 19 Louie Psihoyos/Corbis. 15T Royalty-Free/Corbis. 24B, 25 The Natural History Museum, London.
27B Roger Harris/Science Photo Library. 18 Larry Miller/Science Photo Library. 13 Sinclair Stammers/Science Photo Library.
7T, 10, 11T, 12T, 12B, 14BFL 27CR, 28FL, 28R, 28FR Ticktock Media Archive.
Front cover: TR Lisa Alderson, C Simon Mendez, BFL Simon Mendez, BCL and BCR Ticktock Media Archive, BFL Shutterstock
Back cover: TL Lisa Alderson, BL Simon Mendez

Every effort has been made to trace the copyright holders and we apologise in advance for any unintentional omissions.
We would be pleased to insert the appropriate acknowledgement in any subsequent edition of this publication.

Contents

Let's Start Digging

You have an exciting job. You're a dinosaur expert! Dinosaurs lived millions of years ago. You try to find their bones, eggs and footprints. You use these clues to help you discover how dinosaurs lived. Then you tell everybody else what you have discovered!

What does a dinosaur expert do?

Look for bones that have been buried for millions of years.

Write about your finds and read what other scientists have written.

Show your dinosaur discoveries in a museum.

Sometimes you talk to children about your job.

But did you know that dinosaur experts sometimes have to use maths?

In this book you will find lots of number puzzles that dinosaur experts have to solve every day. You will also get the chance to answer lots of number questions about bones and fossils and find out a lot about dinosaurs, too.

What's inside the book?

Find out what needs to be done next in your busy day.

The charts and tables will help you answer the maths questions.

Answer the questions and practise your maths skills.

Look out for facts about dinosaurs.

If you get stuck, there are some tips to help you on pages 30-31.

A New Display

You are planning some new displays for the museum. One is about what the weather was like and what dinosaurs ate. Firstly, you have to decide how the display will look.

Visitors to the museum want to know what the weather was like at the time of the dinosaurs. You show them how to make a weather chart.

1. How many days are wet on this weather chart?

	Weather
KEY	
sunny	Day 1
	Day 2
	Day 3
cloudy	Day 4
rainy	Day 5
	Day 6
	Day 7

There was no grass in dinosaur times. But there were lots of ferns for plant-eating dinosaurs to eat.

2. If 20 ferns were shared between 4 dinosaurs, how many ferns would each dinosaur get?

3. A herd of plant-eating dinosaurs could eat its way through the ferns very quickly. If the herd ate 3 metres of ferns in 1 hour, how many metres of ferns would it eat in 3 hours?

20

4. Many fossils of dinosaur dung, called coprolites, have been found. Scientists study these to find out what different dinosaurs ate. You have a collection of 35 coprolites and decide to put 15 on display. How many are left?

In the time of the dinosaurs the world looked very different. The weather at the time of the dinosaurs may have been very hot and wet.

21

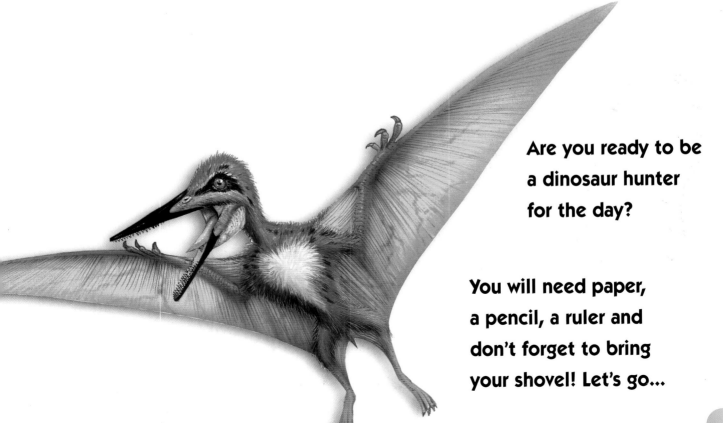

Are you ready to be a dinosaur hunter for the day?

You will need paper, a pencil, a ruler and don't forget to bring your shovel! Let's go...

Walking with Dinosaurs

Hunting dinosaurs is not as difficult as you might think. Dinosaurs roamed the Earth millions of years ago. They have left a lot behind them, including footprints, eggs and bones. Today you are going on a journey to search for dinosaur bones in North America.

The time when dinosaurs lived is divided into three different periods.

- **Cretaceous Period**
- **Jurassic Period**
- **Triassic Period**

This map shows some places where dinosaur fossils have been found.

Map of Canada and the United States

1 How many Triassic sites are there?

2 Which period has the most sites?

Here are some dinosaurs that lived in the different periods.

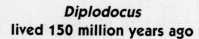

Diplodocus
lived 150 million years ago

Liliensternus
lived 220 million years ago

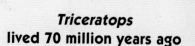

Triceratops
lived 70 million years ago

3 Which dinosaur lived longest ago?

You have arrived at a site in the desert where the ground is dry and rocky. You know dinosaurs used to live here. Suddenly you see a giant footprint.

4 Look at this dinosaur footprint next to a hand. How many hands do you think might fit across this footprint?

1   2 to 3   more than 3

Some dinosaurs went around in groups called herds. This helped to protect them from enemies. A herd may have been very large. Fossil hunters have found up to 30 dinosaur skeletons in one place.

5 Try making 30 by adding the same number many times. 30 is
30 ones   3 tens   how many twos?

Amargasaurus may have travelled in herds. This dinosaur was 9 metres long with two rows of spines down its neck.

Whose Footprint?

You have to find out which dinosaur made this footprint. You look it up in a book. It looks like the footprint of *Iguanodon*. This dinosaur usually moved on all four feet but it could also stand on just its back feet. This made *Iguanodon* different from other dinosaurs.

1 *Iguanodon* had three toes on each of its feet. Its front feet also had a thumb and a spike for holding plants. How many toes did *Iguanodon* have all together?

2 *Iguanodon* was 10 metres long from the tip of its nose to the end of its tail. If its tail was 3 metres long, how long would the rest of it be?

A dinosaur footprint, showing the three toes of the back foot.

You find three more footprints, and you decide to make some plaster casts to take back to the museum.

Instructions

1. Mix the plaster with some water.
   Use 1 litre of water for 1 pack of plaster.
2. Pour the mixture into the footprint.
3. Wait 5 minutes for the plaster to dry.
4. Ease out the plaster cast.

3 It takes you 15 minutes to make each plaster cast. How much of this time is spent waiting for the plaster to dry?

$\frac{1}{2}$ $\frac{1}{4}$ $\frac{1}{3}$

4 How many litres of water do you need if you use 3 packs of plaster?

5 If you make 8 plaster casts of each of the front feet and 3 of each of the back feet, how many casts will you have in total?

6 Now you draw a plan to show where you found each footprint. Starting from the back left footprint, which footprint did you find 2 squares up and 2 squares right?

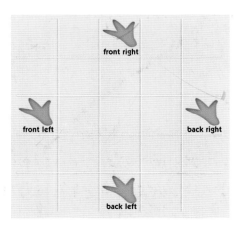

Bony Clues

You collect other bits of bone that you find. Then you spot something half buried in the sand. You hurry towards it, careful not to tread on any other fossils. It looks as if it might be part of the leg of the dinosaur *Stegosaurus*.

Stegosaurus was 9 metres long. It had two lines of plates along its back. At the end of its tail it had 4 long, sharp spikes which it could swing at attackers.

1 One of the bits of bone you find is 50 centimetres long. If this is half of the bone, how long was the bone?

LENGTH OF BONES

You collect three dinosaur bones. You draw a sketch of them and write the length of the bone underneath.

Front leg bone
1 metre

Hip bone
2 metres

Back leg bone
20 centimetres

2 Put the bones in order from longest to shortest.

Now you have found a tooth – this is very exciting. We know what dinosaurs ate by what their teeth look like. Plant-eaters' teeth were not very sharp. Meat-eaters had very sharp teeth. They were pointed and of different sizes.

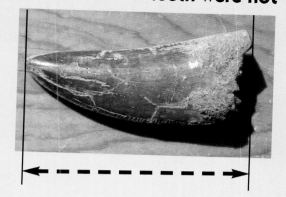

3 Measure this dinosaur tooth with a ruler. What is its length?

You check a chart which tells you which kinds of dinosaurs were meat-eaters and which were plant-eaters.

4 How many dinosaurs in this chart are plant-eaters?

5 How many dinosaurs are there all together?

Plant-eaters	Meat-eaters
Diplodocus	Tyrannosaurus
Stegosaurus	Oviraptor
Triceratops	Velociraptor
Iguanodon	

Tyrannosaurus weighed 6 tonnes. That's the same as over 200 children!

Fossil Finds

Next, you visit some cliffs. This is a good place to find some fossils of sea creatures. You are looking for ammonites, which were alive at the same time as the dinosaurs, and trilobites, which lived millions of years before them.

There were over 10,000 different types of trilobites. They varied in size from 2 cm to 50 cm.

1 Which of the numbers below mean 50 cm?

Half a metre
½ metre
A quarter of a metre
One metre
Fifty centimetres

Trilobites were one of the first animals on Earth.

2 You find three ammonite fossils like this. Each one is 20 cm across. You pack them side by side into a box. How long does your box have to be?

3 You pack another box. This has three rows of fossils with four fossils in each row. How many fossils are in the box?

4 Look at this picture of a rock. How many ammonite fossils do you think are in this picture?

A. about 5

B. about 10

C. about 25

COUNTING YOUR FINDS

5 You find 4 plant fossils, 9 ammonites and 6 trilobites. You draw a block graph to show what you have found. But wait, you have made a mistake. Look at the graph. Can you spot the mistake?

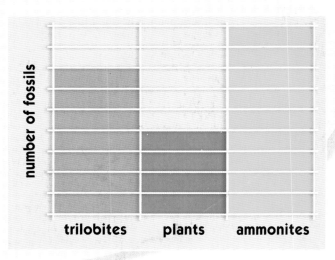

To the Museum

You now have to take your fossils back to the museum. Because you are on a site in the middle of the desert, you are picked up by helicopter and flown back to the museum.

The first thing you see at the museum is the awesome skeleton of the mighty *Tyrannosaurus*. This dinosaur moved around on its hind legs. It had between 50 and 60 teeth. It could easily crush the bones of other dinosaurs.

Tyrannosaurus had a huge head. Its skull was over 1 metre long.

1 Which of these numbers are between 50 and 60?

53   62   75   57   65   49

Tyrannosaurus was big, but it was not the heaviest dinosaur. Many plant-eating dinosaurs weighed much more.

Apatosaurus
30 to 38 tonnes

Triceratops
6 to 12 tonnes

Tyrannosaurus
5 to 7 tonnes

Brachiosaurus
33 to 48 tonnes

2 Put these in order from the lightest dinosaur to the heaviest dinosaur. Use the greatest weight for each kind of dinosaur.

One of your favourite exhibits at the museum is *Apatosaurus*. It took about 10 years for *Apatosaurus* to become fully grown. It may have lived for 100 years in total.

3 How many tens in 100?

Apatosaurus had a huge neck. It could easily reach the tops of trees to eat.

Triceratops was a plant-eater. Its name means "three-horned face." Its 3 horns helped it to defend itself against meat-eaters like Tyrannosaurus.

4 There are 5 *Triceratops* on display, how many horns is that in total?

Triceratops lived in North America. It ate bushes and trees.

Labelling Finds

You take your finds to the museum storeroom. Here you have to label each one. Each bone, tooth, fossil, or footprint is given a label with a code on it.

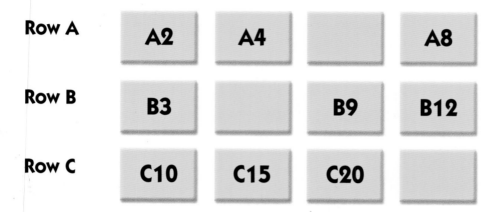

Row A	A2	A4		A8
Row B	B3		B9	B12
Row C	C10	C15	C20	

1 Choose the correct labels below to fill in the gaps in each set above.

A1	C26	B8	B6	A6	C25

**You also have to measure each of your finds.
Here are some of the measuring tools you use.**

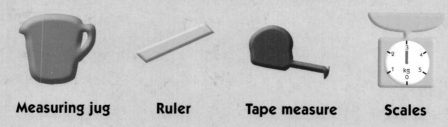

Measuring jug   Ruler   Tape measure   Scales

2 Which tool would you use to measure:
A the length of a bone about the size of your hand?
B the weight of a fossil?
C the length of a hole dug to find fossils?
D water for making a plaster cast?

Stegosaurus might have used its plates to keep warm. It could have stood so that the sun shone on its plates.

You are now putting together a model of *Stegosaurus* for display. The plates to go on the model's back have been labelled. Each plate has been numbered so that it goes in the right place. One row is going to be odd numbers and one row even numbers.

3 Can you sort the plates into the two rows?

7 3 10 2 9 8 1 6 13 11 5 4 12 14

Checking the Fossil Footprint

You unpack the plaster casts you made of the dinosaur footprints. Can you use them to work out more about the dinosaur that made them? You would like to know how tall it was and how fast it was moving.

1 You can work out a dinosaur's height up to its hip, using its footprint. You take the length of the dinosaur footprint and multiply it by 4. The footprints you found are 50 cm long. How high is your dinosaur, up to its hips?

2 You now look at your dinosaur's stride length. This is the distance a dinosaur travels in two steps. Your dinosaur has steps that are 2½ metres long. What is its stride length?

3 With your dinosaur's hip height and stride length you can work out how fast it was moving. Divide the length of stride by its hip height. This gives you a number. Look at this chart. Is your dinosaur running, trotting or walking?

DINOSAUR SPEED

	stride length divided by hip height
walking	under 2
trotting	between 2 and 3
running	over 3

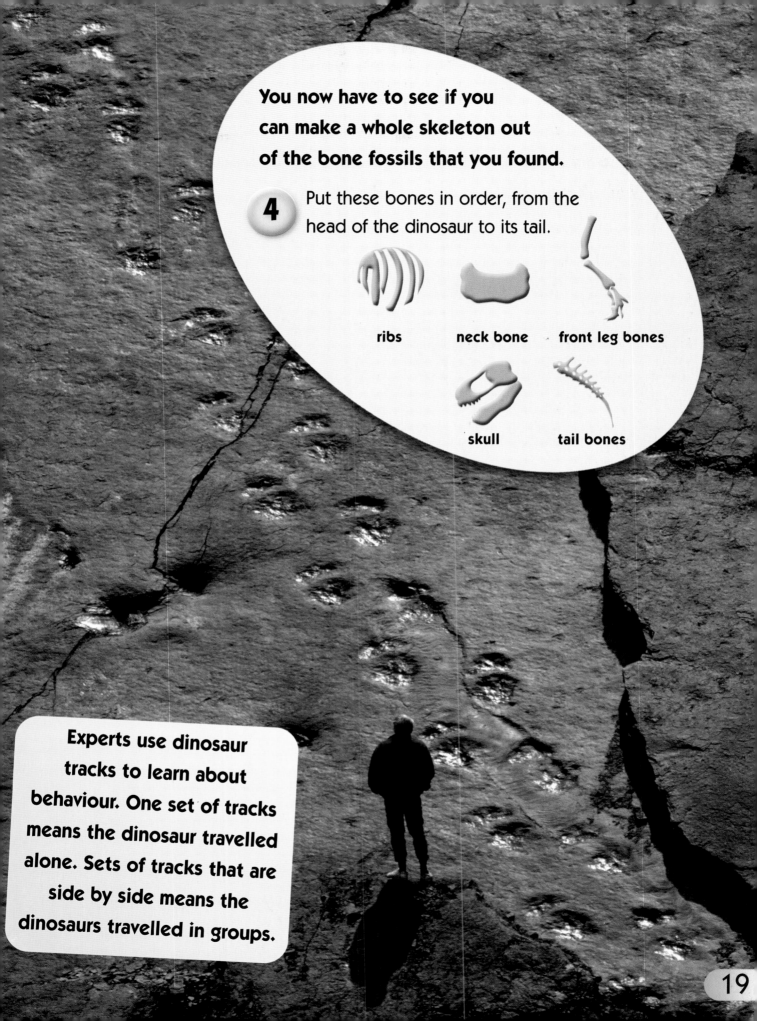

You now have to see if you can make a whole skeleton out of the bone fossils that you found.

4 Put these bones in order, from the head of the dinosaur to its tail.

ribs   neck bone   front leg bones

skull   tail bones

Experts use dinosaur tracks to learn about behaviour. One set of tracks means the dinosaur travelled alone. Sets of tracks that are side by side means the dinosaurs travelled in groups.

A New Display

You are planning some new displays for the museum. One is about what the weather was like and what dinosaurs ate. Firstly, you have to decide how the display will look.

Visitors to the museum want to know what the weather was like at the time of the dinosaurs. You show them how to make a weather chart.

KEY

sunny ☀

cloudy ☁

rainy 🌧

	Weather
Day 1	☀
Day 2	🌧
Day 3	☁
Day 4	🌧
Day 5	☀
Day 6	☁
Day 7	☀

1 How many days are wet on this weather chart?

There was no grass in dinosaur times. But there were lots of ferns for plant-eating dinosaurs to eat.

2 If 20 ferns were shared between 4 dinosaurs, how many ferns would each dinosaur get?

3 A herd of plant-eating dinosaurs could eat its way through the ferns very quickly. If the herd ate 3 metres of ferns in 1 hour, how many metres of ferns would it eat in 3 hours?

4 Many fossils of dinosaur dung, called coprolites, have been found. Scientists study these to find out what different dinosaurs ate. You have a collection of 35 coprolites and decide to put 15 on display. How many are left?

In the time of the dinosaurs the world looked very different. The weather at the time of the dinosaurs may have been very hot and wet.

Flying Visit

One of your favourite subjects is creatures that could fly. *Archaeopteryx* is the oldest known bird. It had feathers and it could fly, although not very well. It was a very fierce hunter.

1 What is the difference between *Archaeopteryx's* length and wingspan?

2 *Archaeopteryx* had three claws on each wing. It used its claws to grasp onto branches. How many wing claws did it have in total?

Here is a chart showing what *Archaeopteryx* measured.

ARCHAEOPTERYX	
Length	30 centimetres
Wingspan	50 centimetres

3 *Archaeopteryx* ate small animals and insects. How many insects are here?

4 *Archaeopteryx* weighed between 300 and 500 grams. If we put *Archaeopteryx* on a scale which of these balances would be correct?

The biggest pterosaur had a wingspan of about 12 metres.

During dinosaur times there were some reptiles that could fly. They were called pterosaurs.

5 This pterosaur has made a quarter turn in a clockwise direction. Which picture is correct?

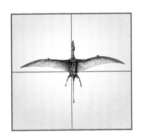 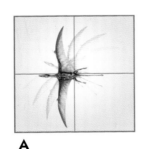 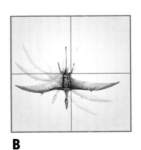 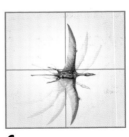

A   B   C

6 Your star fossil is now going on display. It is a *Pterodactylus*. This flying reptile had a wingspan of 2 metres. Its body was half as long as its wingspan. Which is the correct display label?

PTERODACTYLUS

Habitat: rivers and seas
Wingspan: 20 cm
Body length: 10 cm

Label A

PTERODACTYLUS

Habitat: rivers and seas
Wingspan: 200 cm
Body length: 50 cm

Label B

PTERODACTYLUS

Habitat: rivers and seas
Wingspan: 200 cm
Body length: 100 cm

Label C

Dinosaur Parents

Dinosaurs laid eggs. You decide to put on a display showing a dinosaur nest with some eggs.

The eggs of *Hypselosaurus* were laid in a line as the dinosaur walked along. These eggs are not in order. One is not there.

1 Which one is missing?

2 8 12 4 6 10 9 13 1 3 7 5

Some dinosaur eggs were very big indeed. The eggs of *Hypselosaurus* were like footballs, at least 30 centimetres across.

2 If you filled a *Hypselosaurus* egg with water it could hold about two litres. How many millilitres is that?

Maiasaura lived in groups. The group stayed near the eggs until the babies hatched. Each mother laid between 15 and 20 eggs.

3 Which of these numbers are between 15 and 20?

17 12 25 52 10 16 19

Some dinosaurs made nests and sat on their eggs to keep them warm, just like birds today. *Oviraptor* was one of these.

4 Look at these hatched dinosaur eggs.
Find the pieces that fit together to make whole eggs.

A

B

C

D

E

F

G

H

Oviraptor was about
2 metres long and
walked on two legs.

Is this a Record?

You have been asked to make a list of dinosaur record breakers.
New dinosaur fossils are being found all the time so records have to
be kept up-to-date.

LONGEST

The longest dinosaurs were gigantic. They ate plants and they moved slowly.
Seismosaurus
was among
the longest.

1 *Seismosaurus* was 35 metres long. Do you think that is nearest the length of:
A) a skipping rope? **B)** a bus? **C)** 3 buses?

2 Meat-eating dinosaurs were not so long, but one of the longest was
Tyrannosaurus. It was 12 metres long. Do you think that is nearest the length of:
A) a skipping rope? **B)** a bus? **C)** 3 buses?

TALLEST

The tallest dinosaurs, like *Brachiosaurus*,
had long necks. They could reach up to
eat the leaves at the top of tall trees.

3 *Brachiosaurus* was about 25 metres tall. If you and your friends stood on
each other's shoulders until you were as tall as *Brachiosaurus*, about how
many children would there be?

5, 25, or 100?

SMALLEST

One of the smallest dinosaurs was *Bambiraptor*. This dinosaur was only 1 metre long and weighed about 3 kilograms.

4 Which of these may weigh the same as *Bambiraptor*?

an egg

a shoe

a bag of potatoes

Some meat-eating dinosaurs were quite small. *Velociraptor* was about 2 metres long – and half of this length was its tail.

In the Shop

All your displays are now ready for the Grand Opening tomorrow. On your way out you go into the museum gift shop. You like the model insects inside see-through blocks.

The museum has some real insects from dinosaur times. The insects got trapped in sticky stuff from trees called resin. The resin became hard and turned into amber.

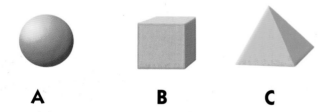

A   B   C

A piece of amber showing insects which were trapped millions of years ago.

1 Here are some plastic models of the amber. What are the names of these shapes?

2 A plastic model costs £1.50. You give the cashier £2. How much change will you get?

3 Which of these fossils is the most expensive?

A   B   C   D

£3   75p   £2.50   £3.75

Brachiosaurus was 12 metres tall, about the height of a 4-storey building.

4 Look at the poster on the right. How much money do you save if you go on the Grand Opening day?

5 You bring two friends to the Grand Opening. How much will the entrance fee cost all together?

6 You love the exhibition! You go once for the Grand Opening and twice later. How much do you pay all together?

Meet Allosaurus
and other dinosaurs!

Entrance fee.......................... £4

Entrance fee on
Grand Opening day............. £3

Tips and Help

PAGES 6-7

Putting numbers in order – To put these numbers of years in order, try looking at the 'hundreds' first, so 150 has one hundred, 220 has two hundreds and 70 has no (zero) hundreds. In order the longest ago is 220 million years, then 150 million years, and 70 million years is the most recent.

PAGES 8-9

Subtraction – If we take away the length of *Iguanodon*'s tail from its total body length we are doing a subtraction.

Fractions – A fraction is part of a whole. When we share or cut something into two equal parts each part is the fraction ½ (half). If it is cut into three equal parts each is the fraction ⅓ (a third) and in four equal parts each would be ¼ (a quarter).

PAGES 10-11

Putting measures in order – Check that the measures are all made in the same unit of measurement. Here you can change them all to centimetres. Remember there are 100 centimetres in one metre.

Measuring length – When you use a ruler, place the '0' (zero) on one end of the line you are measuring. Then you can 'read off' what it measures at the other end of the line.

PAGES 12-13

Metres and centimetres – There are 100 centimetres in one metre and 50 centimetres in half a metre.

Rows and columns – 3 rows, each of 4 fossils, gives the same total as 4 rows, each of 3 fossils.

Estimates – When you say how many ammonites you think there are in the picture, this is an estimate. Careful estimates are useful when doing maths.

PAGES 14-15

Numbers between – To work out where numbers fit, think of a number line, order the numbers along it. Then you will see where they fit. Here your number line looks like this: So only two numbers fit along your number line.

| 50 | 51 | 52 | 53 | 54 | 55 | 56 | 57 | 58 | 59 | 60 |

Lots of three – This is the same as counting in threes or the products in the three times table. It is good to remember them:
0 3 6 9 12 15 18 21 24 27 30 33 36

PAGES 16-17

Measuring tools – It is important to choose the right measuring tool for a job. Remember that a jug is used to measure liquids, and scales are used to measure weight. A ruler and a tape measure are tools for measuring height, width and length.

Odds and evens – Even numbers are the numbers in the counting pattern of twos: 2 4 6 8 10 12 14 16 18 20…. and so on. Odd numbers are the numbers not in this pattern; that is 1 3 5 7 9 11 13 15 17 19…. and so on.

PAGES 18-19

Multiplying and dividing – We can see how these are connected:
$2 \times 2\frac{1}{2} = 5$ and $5 \div 2 = 2\frac{1}{2}$

PAGES 20-21

Sharing – Sharing is the same as doing division. We can find out either how many are to have a share, or the size of each share. Here it is the number of ferns for each dinosaur (that is how many in each share).

PAGES 22-23

Kilograms and grams – 1 kilogram is 1000 grams.

A ¼ turn – There are four quarter turns in one complete turn.

Clockwise – The direction in which the hands of a clock move.

clockwise

anti clockwise

PAGES 24-25

Litres and millilitres – 1 litre is 1000 millilitres.

PAGES 26-27

Longest, smallest, tallest – Remember we say 'longer', 'smaller', or 'taller' when we compare two things, and 'longest', 'smallest' and 'tallest' when we compare three or more than three things. Here we are comparing lots of dinosaurs.

PAGES 28-29

Money – One pound is 100 pence.

Answers

PAGES 6-7

1 6
2 Cretaceous
3 *Liliensternus*
4 2 to 3
5 15 twos

PAGES 8-9

1 12
2 7 metres
3 ⅓
4 3 litres
5 22 plaster casts
6 back right footprint

PAGES 10-11

1 1 metre
2 hip bone, front leg bone, back leg bone
3 6 centimetres
4 4
5 7

PAGES 12-13

1 half a metre, ½ metre and fifty centimetres
2 60 centimetres
3 12
4 about 10 trilobites
5 graph shows 7 trilobites

PAGES 14-15

1 53 and 57
2 *Tyrannosaurus, Triceratops, Apatosaurus* and
   Brachiosaurus
3 10
4 15 horns

PAGES 16-17

1 Row A - A6
   Row B - B6
   Row C - C25
2 A - ruler
   B - scales
   C - tape measure
   D - measuring jug
3 2, 4, 6, 8, 10, 12 and 14
   1, 3, 5, 7, 9, 11 and 13

PAGES 18-19

1 2 metres
2 5 metres
3 trotting
4 skull, neck bone, front leg bone, ribs, tail bone

PAGES 20-21

1 2 days
2 5 ferns
3 9 metres
4 20 coprolites

PAGES 22-23

1 20 centimetres
2 6 claws
3 16 insects
4 B
5 C
6 Label C

PAGES 24-25

1 11
2 2000 ml
3 16, 17 and 19
4 A and D
   B and E
   C and H
   F and G

PAGES 26-27

1 C - 3 buses
2 B - 1 bus
3 25 children
4 bag of potatoes

PAGES 28-29

1 A - sphere
   B - cube
   C - pyramid
2 50 pence
3 D
4 £1
5 £9
6 £11